■SCHOLASTIC

M000035689

Comprehension Skills
40 Short Passages for Close Reading

GRADE **6**

Linda Ward Beech

New York • Toronto • London • Auckland • Sydney
Mexico City • New Delhi • Hong Kong • Buenos Aires

Teaching *Resources*

The reading passages in this book were selected and adapted from the following titles in the series,
35 Reading Passages for Comprehension: *Context Clues & Figurative Language, Inferences & Drawing Conclusions,
Main Ideas & Summarizing,* and *Point of View & Fact and Opinion* (Scholastic, 2006).
Copyright © 2006 by Linda Ward Beech.

Cover design by Jorge J. Namerow
Interior design by Jason Robinson
Illustrations by Mike Gordon

ISBN: 978-0-545-46057-6
Text copyright © 2012 by Linda Ward Beech
Illustrations copyright © 2012 by Scholastic Inc.
Published by Scholastic Inc.
All rights reserved.
Printed in the U.S.A.

7 8 9 10   40   19 18 17

Contents

Passages

Using This Book

Reading comprehension in nonfiction involves numerous thinking skills. Students require these skills to make sense of a text and become successful readers. This book offers practice in key skills needed to meet the Common Core State Standards in Reading/Language Arts for grade six. (See page 6 for more.) Each student page includes a short passage focusing on four of these essential comprehension skills.

Comprehension Skills At-a-Glance

Use the information that follows to introduce the reading comprehension skills covered in this book.

Main Idea & Details

Understanding the main or key idea of a paragraph is crucial for a reader. The main idea is what the paragraph is about. The other parts of the paragraph help to explain more about this key idea. The main idea is sometimes in the first or last sentence of a paragraph. Students should be aware that some main ideas are stated explicitly and others are implicit requiring readers to put together details to determine the main idea.

The information that supports the main idea is usually referred to as the details. Details—facts, examples, definitions, etc.—help a reader gain a fuller understanding of a paragraph.

Summarize

Readers should be able to use main ideas to summarize a text. By summarizing, students are better able to recall important points. This is an important skill for taking notes and studying for exams.

Context Clues

Using context clues means determining an unfamiliar word's meaning by studying the phrases, sentences, and overall text with which the word appears. Context clues help readers comprehend and enjoy a text and also read more smoothly and efficiently.

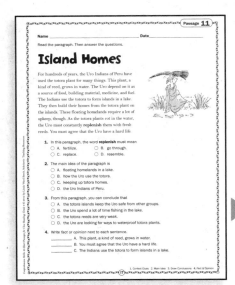

In this paragraph, students have to read the entire text and ask themselves "What is this paragraph mainly about?" The main idea is supported by different facts (details) about how egg sizes are determined.

Several clues in the paragraph (*upkeep*, *rot*, *fresh reeds*) help a reader determine the meaning of *replenish*.

Figurative Language

Beyond using context clues to derive meaning is the ability to differentiate between literal and figurative language. Readers who can recognize figures of speech and determine their meanings are well on their way to fluency.

Inference

Although some students don't know what an inference is, many are most likely making inferences—both in their daily lives and when reading—without being aware of it. Students should understand that writers don't include every detail in their writing; it is up to readers to supply some information. A reader makes a guess or inference by putting together what is in a text with what he or she already knows. Inferring makes a significant difference in how much a reader gains from a text.

Draw Conclusions

After thinking about information in a text, a reader makes a decision or conclusion by examining evidence rooted in the text. Students should know that writers don't always state all of their ideas, so readers have to look for clues to understand what is meant.

Fact & Opinion

Readers who can identify and differentiate between statements of fact and opinion are better able to analyze and assess a text. Students should learn to recognize phrases, such as *I think, you should,* and *it's the best/most,* that signal opinions.

Point of View

While distinguishing fact from opinion is one step in the reading process, it is important for students to go further. They should be able to sort facts, opinions, and feelings to help determine a writer's point of view and compare it to what they themselves think. Students should learn that good readers consult several sources on subjects of interest to gain different points of view.

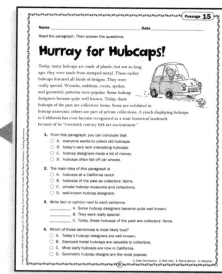

Students have to read closely to answer the inference question, "Which of these sentences is most likely true?"

To appreciate this text, the reader should understand that the writer has inserted commentary or opinion into the paragraph. For example, the sentence, *They are incredible creatures,* is the author's opinion.

Tips

★ Tell students to first read the passage and then answer the questions. Show them how to fill in the circles for bubble-test questions.

★ The comprehension skills targeted in the questions accompanying each passage are labeled at the bottom of the page.

★ Review the completed pages with students on a regular basis. Encourage them to explain their thinking for each correct answer.

Meeting the Common Core State Standards

The passages and comprehension questions in this book are designed to help you meet both your specific English/Language Arts standards and learning expectations as well as those recommended by the Common Core State Standards Initiative (CCSSI). The activities in this book align with the following CCSSI standards for grade six.

Reading Standards for Informational Text

Key Ideas and Details

1. Cite textual evidence to support analysis of what the text says explicitly as well as inferences drawn from the text.
2. Determine a central idea of a text and how it is conveyed through particular details; provide a summary of the text distinct from personal opinions or judgments.

Craft and Structure

4. Determine the meaning of words and phrases as they are used in a text, including figurative, connotative, and technical meanings.
5. Analyze how a particular sentence fits into the overall structure of a text and contributes to the development of the ideas.
6. Determine an author's point of view or purpose in a text and explain how it is conveyed in the text.

Integration of Knowledge and Ideas

8. Trace and evaluate the argument and specific claims in a text, distinguishing claims that are supported by reasons and evidence from claims that are not.

Range of Reading and Level of Text Complexity

10. By the end of the year, read and comprehend literary nonfiction in the grades 6–8 text complexity band proficiently, with scaffolding as needed at the high end of the range.

Language Standards

Knowledge of Language

3. Use knowledge of language and its conventions when writing, speaking, reading, or listening.

Vocabulary Acquisition and Use

4. Determine or clarify the meaning of unknown and multiple-meaning words and phrases based on *grade 6 reading and content*, choosing flexibly from a range of strategies.
    a. Use context as a clue to the meaning of a word or phrase.
    d. Verify the preliminary determination of the meaning of a word or phrase.
5. Demonstrate understanding of figurative language, word relationships, and nuances in word meanings.
    a. Interpret figures of speech in context.
    b. Use the relationship between particular words to better understand each of the words.
    c. Distinguish among the connotations (associations) of words with similar denotations (definitions).
6. Acquire and use accurately grade-appropriate general academic and domain-specific words and phrases; gather vocabulary knowledge when considering a word or phrase important to comprehension or expression.

Comprehension Skills: 40 Short Passages for Close Reading, Grade 6 © 2012 by Linda Ward Beech, Scholastic Teaching Resources

Name _____ Date _____

Read the paragraph. Then answer the questions.

Crazy Records

Ashrita Furman likes to break records. In fact, over the years Furman has set or broken more than 79 records listed in the *Guinness Book of World Records.* Two of his **feats** include race-walking the fastest mile while twirling a hula hoop, and walking 81 miles with a milk bottle on top of his head. He has also held records for balancing 75 glasses on his chin and for going up and down Mt. Fuji in Japan on a pogo stick. Why? Mr. Furman feels these activities bring him inner peace.

1. The main idea of this paragraph is
- ○ A. *The Guinness Book of World Records.*
- ○ B. Climbing Japan's Mt. Fuji.
- ○ C. How to walk with a bottle on your head.
- ◉ D. Ashrita Furman likes to break records.

2. Reread the paragraph. Write a supporting detail for the main idea.

_____

_____

3. Which sentence is most likely *not* true?
- ○ A. Mr. Furman has good balance.
- ○ B. Mr. Furman enjoys his fame.
- ○ C. Mr. Furman is in poor health.
- ○ D. Mr. Furman works hard at his records.

4. In this paragraph, the word **feats** means
- ○ A. what you walk on.
- ○ B. broken records.
- ○ C. accomplishments.
- ○ D. balancing acts.

1. Main Idea   2. Details   3. Inference   4. Context Clues

Name _____ Date _____

Read the paragraph. Then answer the questions..

Buying Eggs

Consumers often spend a few puzzled moments looking at egg cartons in supermarkets. That's because there are six official egg sizes. The sizes are determined by weight. A jumbo, the largest-size egg, weighs 30 ounces, while a peewee egg, the smallest size, weighs only 15 ounces. In between are extra-large, large, medium, and small eggs. Most markets only stock the four largest sizes; small and peewee eggs are usually sold to bakers and companies in the food processing business.

1. The title that best summarizes this paragraph is
   - ● A. Official Egg Sizes.
   - ○ B. Puzzling Consumers.
   - ○ C. Opening Egg Cartons.
   - ○ D. Eggs for Bakeries.

2. From this paragraph, you can conclude that
   - ○ A. the largest eggs are the best ones.
   - ○ B. hens try to lay heavy eggs.
   - ● C. consumers don't know how eggs are sized.
   - ○ D. egg cartons hold different size eggs.

3. The main idea of this paragraph is
   - ○ A. how small eggs are used.
   - ○ B. how egg sizes are determined.
   - ○ C. why eggs are different sizes.
   - ● D. why there are only six egg sizes.

4. Which word best describes the writer's point of view?
   - ○ A. absorbed
   - ○ B. argumentative
   - ● C. informed

1. Summarize 2. Draw Conclusions 3. Main Idea 4. Point of View

Name _____ **Date** _____

Read the paragraph. Then answer the questions.

Daniel Webster's Program

In 1829, Daniel Webster started a page program in the United States Senate. The pages are young people who work for the senators. For example, pages run errands and deliver messages. Pages are chosen by the senators of their home states. They must be 16 years old, have good grades, and show leadership qualities. Pages live near the Capitol Building and attend school. They are **exempted** from homework when the senators work overtime. Pages get paid, but the biggest reward is the experience of working in the Senate.

1. Fill in the correct circle to show whether each statement is a fact or an inference.

Fact Inference

◯   ◯   A. Pages run errands for senators.

◯   ◯   B. Pages are interested in government.

◯   ◯   C. Pages go to school.

◯   ◯   D. It is an honor to be a Senate page.

2. The main idea of this paragraph is

◯ A. pages run errands and deliver messages.

◯ B. pages must be 16 years of age.

◯ C. the U.S. Senate page program.

◯ D. pay for Senate pages.

3. From this paragraph, you can conclude that Webster's program

◯ A. is a good way to get out of doing homework.

◯ B. benefits both senators and pages.

◯ C. pays pages high salaries.

◯ D. offers a lot of sports activities to pages.

4. In this paragraph, the word **exempted** means

◯ A. excited.   ◯ B. excused.

◯ C. charged.   ◯ D. overworked.

1. Inference   2. Main Idea   3. Draw Conclusions   4. Context Clues

Name _____ **Date**_____

Read the paragraph. Then answer the questions.

Clues for a Hobby

What is letterboxing? It's a very cool hobby
that has grown in popularity in recent years.
To get started you need a notebook, an ink
pad, a compass, and good walking shoes.
Most people check a Web site to obtain clues
telling how to find letterboxes. Each letterbox is a container holding a rubber stamp and a
notebook. Letterboxes are hidden in public places such as parks or woods. When seekers find
a letterbox, they add its stamp to their notebook. Most letterbox fans also carry their own
stamps, which they stamp into the notebook in the letterbox. This is called "stamping in."

1. From this paragraph, you can conclude that
   - ○ A. everyone enjoys the hobby of letterboxing.
   - ○ B. letterboxing is an ancient tradition.
   - ○ C. people trespass a lot when letterboxing.
   - ○ D. letterboxing is like an outdoor detective game.

2. The title that best summarizes this paragraph is
   - ○ A. Looking for a Letterbox.
   - ○ B. What You'll find in a Letterbox.
   - ○ C. Learning About Letterboxing.
   - ○ D. Stamping Letterbox Notebooks.

3. Which sentence is most likely *not* true?
   - ○ A. Letterbox fans collect stamps.
   - ○ B. Letterbox fans do a lot of walking.
   - ○ C. The Internet is important in letterboxing.
   - ○ D. Letterbox fans all have the same stamp.

4. Reread the paragraph. Write the writer's opinion about letterboxing.
   Then write a fact that the writer gives.

   _____

   _____

   _____

Comprehension Skills: 40 Short Passages for Close Reading, Grade 6 © 2012 by Linda Ward Beech, Scholastic Teaching

Name _____ **Date** _____

Read the paragraph. Then answer the questions.

Big Business

Where do you build the world's largest jet airliner? First, you have to put up the world's largest building. That's just what happened in Everett, Washington. An airplane factory there covers more than 98 acres under one roof. More than 75 NFL football fields could fit inside! More than 15 railcars a day deliver parts to the factory. Workers use overhead cranes and forklifts to assemble the large pieces. Buyers from all over the world purchase the finished airplanes.

1. The main idea of this paragraph is
- ○ A. looking for the largest jet airliner.
- ○ B. railcars deliver parts to the factory.
- ○ C. the largest building is a jet factory.
- ○ D. how to build airplanes indoors.

2. Reread the paragraph. Find and write a detail that supports the main idea.

_____

_____

3. Which word best reflects the writer's point of view?
- ○ A. appalled
- ○ B. awed
- ○ C. relieved

4. From this paragraph, you can conclude that
- ○ A. only one plane is assembled at one time.
- ○ B. cranes do most of the work in the factory.
- ○ C. workers arrive at the factory by train.
- ○ D. many parts are made in other places.

1. Main Idea 2. Details 3. Point of View 4. Draw Conclusions

Name _____ Date_____

Read the paragraph. Then answer the questions.

Long-Ago Lighthouse

Sailors have always needed lighthouses to warn them of
dangerous conditions. The first tower that was built for
such a purpose was at the entrance to Port Alexandria,
a long-ago capital of ancient Egypt. The tower, called
Pharos, was a mighty giant. It was so impressive a
structure that it was known as one of the seven wonders
of the ancient world. Fire beacons burning on the tower
helped ships navigate through the **treacherous** waters
approaching the city.

1. The title that best summarizes this paragraph is
   - ○ A. Burning Fire Beacons in the Night.
   - ○ B. Helping Ships Navigate Tricky Waters.
   - ○ C. Pharos, the First Lighthouse Tower.
   - ○ D. A Look at Ancient Egypt.

2. In this paragraph, the word **treacherous** means
   - ○ A. tremendous.   ○ B. disloyal.
   - ○ C. deceptive.   ○ D. dark.

3. Which sentence is most likely *not* true?
   - ○ A. Ships often wrecked approaching Alexandria.
   - ○ B. Alexandria was a busy port city.
   - ○ C. Pharos was known to sailors in the ancient world.
   - ○ D. All the wonders of the ancient world were in Egypt.

4. Reread the paragraph. Find and write a sentence that is an example of a metaphor.

   _____

   _____

1. Summarize 2. Context Clues 3. Inference 4. Figurative Language

Comprehension Skills: 40 Short Passages for Close Reading, Grade 6 © 2012 by Linda Ward Beech, Scholastic Teaching Resources

Name _____ Date_____

Read the paragraph. Then answer the questions.

Island Homes

For hundreds of years, the Uro Indians of Peru have used the totora plant for many things. This plant, a kind of reed, grows in water. The Uro depend on it as a source of food, building material, medicine, and fuel. The Indians use the totora to form islands in a lake. They then build their homes from the totora plant on the islands. These floating homelands require a lot of upkeep, though. As the totora plants rot in the water, the Uro must constantly **replenish** them with fresh reeds. You must agree that the Uro have a hard life.

1. In this paragraph, the word **replenish** must mean
  - ○ A. fertilize.
  - ○ B. go through.
  - ○ C. replace.
  - ○ D. resemble.

2. The main idea of the paragraph is
  - ○ A. floating homelands in a lake.
  - ○ B. how the Uro use the totora.
  - ○ C. keeping up totora homes.
  - ○ D. the Uro Indians of Peru.

3. From this paragraph, you can conclude that
  - ○ A. the totora islands keep the Uro safe from other groups.
  - ○ B. the Uro spend a lot of time fishing in the lake.
  - ○ C. the totora reeds are very weak.
  - ○ D. the Uro are looking for ways to waterproof totora plants.

4. Write *fact* or *opinion* next to each sentence.
  - _____ A. This plant, a kind of reed, grows in water.
  - _____ B. You must agree that the Uro have a hard life.
  - _____ C. The Indians use the totora to form islands in a lake.

1. Context Clues 2. Main Idea 3. Draw Conclusions 4. Fact & Opinion

Name _____ Date_____

Read the paragraph. Then answer the questions.

Capturing Harlem

<u>The camera spoke for him</u>. In the 1920s and '30s James Van DerZee photographed the people and events in Harlem, a part of New York City. At that time, Harlem was home to talented black entertainers, artists, poets, athletes, writers, and politicians. People from all over went to Harlem to enjoy its music, theaters, and nightspots. Van DerZee captured both the famous and the ordinary on film. Many years later, Van DerZee's work was exhibited at an important museum. His photos welcomed people into the past!

1. The underlined words in this paragraph are an example of figurative language called

- ○ A. metaphor.
- ○ B. personification.
- ○ C. simile.
- ○ D. hyperbole.

2. The title that best summarizes this paragraph is

- ○ A. Events and People in Harlem.
- ○ B. A Harlem Museum.
- ○ C. The Work of James Van DerZee.
- ○ D. The Famous and Ordinary on Film.

3. Which word best reflects the writer's point of view?

- ○ A. angry
- ○ B. detached
- ○ C. pleased

4. Which sentence is most likely *not* true?

- ○ A. Harlem was a fascinating place in the 1920s and '30s.
- ○ B. James Van DerZee was a gifted photographer.
- ○ C. James Van DerZee had a talking camera.
- ○ D. Van DerZee's work recorded Harlem history.

Name _____ Date_____

Read the paragraph. Then answer the questions.

Running With Haruurara

Fans love racehorses that win. Curiously, a horse in Japan became a favorite for losing. The horse, named Haruurara, ran more than 100 races—and lost them all. Then a news story featured this four-legged loser. Suddenly, Haruurara had lots of devoted fans. <u>The horse was a lucky charm</u>. The Japanese thought if they lost with Haruurara, they wouldn't lose other things, such as their jobs or homes. So backing a racing loser became popular. Some would say it was a no-win situation!

1. Which phrase best reflects the writer's point of view?
- ○ A. amused by the unusual story
- ○ B. angered by the horse's losses
- ○ C. shocked by the idea of lucky charms

2. The main idea of this paragraph is
- ○ A. a favorite Japanese horse.
- ○ B. a horse that couldn't run.
- ○ C. backing a racing loser in Japan.
- ○ D. losing 100 horse races.

3. The underlined words in this paragraph are an example of figurative language called
- ○ A. metaphor.   ○ B. personification.
- ○ C. simile.   ○ D. hyperbole.

4. From this paragraph, you can conclude that
- ○ A. Many Japanese are a bit superstitious.
- ○ B. Haruurara lost on purpose.
- ○ C. Haruurara was a good racehorse.
- ○ D. the Japanese don't care about winning.

Name _____ **Date**_____

Read the paragraph. Then answer the questions.

Up the Amazon

Most surfers find their waves in the ocean, but in Brazil, surfers find them in the Amazon River. Each March and April, when the river waters are highest, strong tides from the Atlantic Ocean push into the Amazon basin. These tides create a giant **swell** that travels upstream for hundreds of miles at speeds of 20 miles an hour. Brazilians call this endless wave a *pororoca*. Surfing for miles up the river is much more fun than a short ocean ride. All surfers should try this unique challenge.

1. Write *fact* or *opinion* next to each sentence.
   _____ A. Brazilians call this endless wave a *pororoca*.
   _____ B. All surfers should try this unique challenge.
   _____ C. Surfing for miles up the river is much more fun than a short ocean ride.

2. The title that best summarizes this paragraph is
   ○ A. Surfing the Amazon River.
   ○ B. From the Atlantic to the Amazon.
   ○ C. Tides of 20 Miles an Hour.
   ○ D. Surfers in Brazil.

3. The word that best reflects the writer's point of view is
   ○ A. critical.
   ○ B. wondering.
   ○ C. certain.

4. In this paragraph, the word **swell** means
   ○ A. really great.
   ○ B. unbroken wave.
   ○ C. sea creature.
   ○ D. large boat.

Name _____ Date_____

Read the paragraph. Then answer the questions.

Hurray for Hubcaps!

Today, many hubcaps are made of plastic, but not so long ago, they were made from stamped metal. These earlier hubcaps featured all kinds of designs. They were really special. Wreaths, emblems, crests, spokes, and geometric patterns were popular. Some hubcap designers became quite well known. Today, these hubcaps of the past are collectors' items. Some are exhibited in hubcap museums; others are part of private collections. A ranch displaying hubcaps in California has even become recognized as a state historical landmark because of its "twentieth century folk art environment."

1. From this paragraph, you can conclude that
   ○ A. everyone wants to collect old hubcaps.
   ○ B. today's cars lack interesting hubcaps.
   ○ C. hubcap designers made a lot of money.
   ○ D. hubcaps often fall off car wheels.

2. The main idea of this paragraph is
   ○ A. hubcaps at a California ranch.
   ○ B. hubcaps of the past as collectors' items.
   ○ C. private hubcap museums and collections.
   ○ D. well-known hubcap designers.

3. Write *fact* or *opinion* next to each sentence.
   _____ A. Some hubcap designers became quite well known.
   _____ B. They were really special.
   _____ C. Today, these hubcaps of the past are collectors' items.

4. Which of these sentences is most likely true?
   ○ A. Today's hubcap designers are well known.
   ○ B. Stamped metal hubcaps are valuable to collectors.
   ○ C. Most early hubcaps are now in California.
   ○ D. Geometric hubcap designs are the most popular.

1. Draw Conclusions   2. Main Idea   3. Fact & Opinion   4. Inference

Name _____ Date _____

Read the paragraph. Then answer the questions.

Ancient Egyptian Celebrations

People in ancient Egypt celebrated many different kinds of festivals. Some of these honored nature. For example, there were festivals when the Nile River flooded, making the riverbanks **fertile** for farming. Other festivals were celebrated at the beginning of spring and at harvest time. At the celebrations, families enjoyed foods such as watermelon, grapes, and figs that were sold at stalls. People also listened to musicians and watched entertainers such as acrobats.

1. The main idea of this paragraph is
   - ○ A. why the Nile was important to Egypt.
   - ○ B. ancient Egypt had many festivals.
   - ○ C. watermelon was sold at food stalls.
   - ○ D. the festivals honored nature.

2. Reread the paragraph. Write a detail that supports the main idea.

   _____

   _____

3. In this paragraph, the word **fertile** means
   - ○ A. furtive.
   - ○ B. flexible.
   - ○ C. productive.
   - ○ D. festive.

4. From this paragraph, you can conclude that
   - ○ A. the Nile was important to Egyptian farmers.
   - ○ B. Egyptians ate watermelon at all festivals.
   - ○ C. acrobats performed on the Nile's shores.
   - ○ D. nature was always good to the Egyptians.

Name _____ Date _____

Read the paragraph. Then answer the questions.

Traveler of the Past

The explorer Marco Polo left his home in Italy in 1271.
After many years of traveling, his party reached the
summer palace of Kublai Khan in what is now China. Polo
remained at the court for 17 years. He **marveled** at things
not yet seen in Europe. For example, common people
bathed daily. Roads and bridges were paved. People used
paper money instead of gold and silver. The kingdom
had a highly efficient communication system of runners
and horseback riders. When Polo finally returned to
Europe, it took awhile before people believed the stories
he told or the book he wrote about his travels.

1. The title that best summarizes this paragraph is
   ○ A. What Marco Polo Was Like.   ○ B. A Wanderer From Italy.
   ○ C. Meeting Kublai Khan.   ○ D. The Travels of Marco Polo.

2. In this paragraph, the word **marveled** means
   ○ A. showed dismay.   ○ B. showed wonder.
   ○ C. questioned.   ○ D. disregarded.

3. Which sentence is most likely *not* true?
   ○ A. Europeans used gold and silver as currency.
   ○ B. Paper money was easier to carry than gold.
   ○ C. Most roads in Europe were unpaved.
   ○ D. Marco Polo was a prisoner of the Kublai Khan.

4. Reread the paragraph. What was the point of view of Italians toward
   Marco Polo when he returned?

   _____

   _____

Name _____ **Date**_____

Read the paragraph. Then answer the questions.

Skip, Skip

Are you good at skipping stones? Some people have the knack, and others are clueless. Researchers did some tests to see what it takes. First, locate a flat, round stone. When you throw it, add some spin to keep it stable. The heavier the stone, the faster it must be tossed. If it is below a certain **velocity**, the stone will sink. The most important thing is the angle at which the stone hits the water. If it is over 45 degrees, the stone sinks. For the most skips, try for an angle of 20 degrees. That works best.

1. In this paragraph, the word **velocity** must mean
   - ○ A. sea level.
   - ○ B. speed.
   - ○ C. wave height.
   - ○ D. time of day.

2. Write *fact* or *opinion* next to each sentence.
   - _____ A. Some people have the knack, and others are clueless.
   - _____ B. When you throw it, add some spin to keep it stable.
   - _____ C. That works best.

3. The title that best summarizes this paragraph is
   - ○ A. Watch the Angle.
   - ○ B. How to Skip Stones.
   - ○ C. Use a Heavy Stone.
   - ○ D. Use Spin for Skipping.

4. Which word best reflects the writer's point of view?
   - ○ A. outraged
   - ○ B. helpful
   - ○ C. ridiculing

Name _____ Date _____

Read the paragraph. Then answer the questions.

A Great Writer

The language of William Shakespeare is full of figures of speech. In fact, it is Shakespeare's **extraordinary** use of language that made him such a great writer. For example, in the play *The Merry Wives of Windsor*, a character says, "Why then, <u>the world's mine oyster</u>." In another play, called *Antony and Cleopatra*, Cleopatra speaks of her love and respect for Antony with these words: "His legs bestrid the ocean; his reared arm crested the world."

1. The underlined words in this paragraph are an example of figurative language called
   ○ A. metaphor.
   ○ B. personification.
   ○ C. simile.
   ○ D. hyperbole.

2. The word that best reflects the writer's point of view is
   ○ A. frustrated.
   ○ B. condescending.
   ○ C. praising.

3. In this paragraph, the word **extraordinary** means
   ○ A. intense.
   ○ B. normal.
   ○ C. exceptional.
   ○ D. difficult.

4. Reread the paragraph. Write the main idea.

   _____

   _____

Name _____ Date_____

Read the paragraph. Then answer the questions.

Dolphin Stories

Do dolphins and people have a special relationship? Over the centuries, many civilizations have told stories of the bonds between people and dolphins. They are incredible creatures. In an ancient Greek story, the god Dionysus changes some pirates into dolphins. An Australian myth tells about a hero named Gowonda who turns into a helpful dolphin. In a tale from Peru, a pink dolphin sometimes becomes a human. Even today, people report stories of dolphins helping swimmers or guiding ships through dangerous seas.

1. Which phrase best reflects the writer's point of view?
- ○ A. unimpressed by dolphins and their relationship with people
- ○ B. admiration of dolphins and their relationship with people
- ○ C. angry about dolphins and their relationship with people

2. The title that best summarizes the paragraph is
- ○ A. Gowonda the Helpful Dolphin.
- ○ B. Dionysus and Dolphins.
- ○ C. Bonds between People and Dolphins.
- ○ D. A Pink Dolphin from Peru.

3. Write *fact* or *opinion* next to each sentence.

_____ A. In an ancient Greek story, the god Dionysus changes some pirates into dolphins.

_____ B. They are incredible creatures.

_____ C. In a tale from Peru, a pink dolphin sometimes becomes a human.

4. From this paragraph, you can conclude that
- ○ A. people are attracted to dolphins.
- ○ B. dolphins are smarter than people.
- ○ C. dolphins look for swimmers who need help.
- ○ D. dolphins like to guide ships.

Name _____ **Date** _____

Read the paragraph. Then answer the questions.

Thunderhead Memorial

A large granite head looks out of Thunderhead Mountain in South Dakota. The head is magnificent. It is part of a sculpture called the Crazy Horse Memorial, which is being carved from the mountain. Crazy Horse was a Sioux warrior who defeated Lieutenant Colonel George Armstrong Custer at the Battle of Little Bighorn in 1877. The memorial was begun in 1948 by Korzak Ziolkowski. It's taken much too long to complete. When finished, however, it will be 563 feet tall and 641 feet long.

1. Write *fact* or *opinion* next to each sentence.

   _____ A. The memorial was begun in 1948 by Korzak Ziolkowski.

   _____ B. A large granite head rises out of Thunderhead Mountain in South Dakota.

   _____ C. It's taken much too long to complete.

2. Which sentence is most likely *not* true?
   - ○ A. Tourists pay to see the unfinished memorial.
   - ○ B. It's difficult to carve such a memorial.
   - ○ C. It's expensive to create a sculpture from a mountain.
   - ○ D. You can see the memorial from a distance.

3. The phrase that best reflects the writer's point of view is
   - ○ A. mocking about the sculpture.
   - ○ B. fixated by the sculpture.
   - ○ C. impressed by the sculpture.

4. Reread the paragraph. Find and write an example of personification.

   _____

   _____

Name _____ Date _____

Read the paragraph. Then answer the questions.

Ancient Trade Center

Great Zimbabwe, a ruins located within the African country
of Zimbabwe, was a center of trade from the late thirteenth
century to the middle of the fifteenth century. It was also
the home of powerful rulers. Today, scientists are studying
the walls found among the ruins. They are made of smooth
granite and are about 35 feet high and 16 feet deep. No mortar
or plaster was used in building them. That's a remarkable
achievement! Some archaeologists believe that the walls were
built not for defense but to inspire **awe** toward the rulers.

1. Fill in the correct circle to show whether each statement is a fact or an inference.

   Fact   Inference

   ○   ○   A. Great Zimbabwe is located in Africa.

   ○   ○   B. Great Zimbabwe is a place of historic value.

   ○   ○   C. The builders of the walls were skilled.

   ○   ○   D. The walls of Great Zimbabwe reach 35 feet high.

2. In this paragraph, the word **awe** means
   ○ A. obedience.   ○ B. wonder.
   ○ C. awareness.   ○ D. gratitude.

3. The title that best summarizes this paragraph is
   ○ A. Smooth Granite Walls of a Ruin.
   ○ B. Home of Powerful African Rulers.
   ○ C. Ruins of Great Zimbabwe in Africa.
   ○ D. Archaeologists at Work.

4. Reread the paragraph. Find and write a sentence that expresses an opinion.

   _____

   _____

1. Inference   2. Context Clues   3. Summarize   4. Fact & Opinion

Name _____ **Date** _____

Read the paragraph. Then answer the questions.

Elegant Elephants

Elephants don't usually dress up, but some clothing designers thought that these large animals could be quite fashionable. So the designers made some oversize outfits such as tweed suits, a cloak, and some dresses. They even included **gigantic** earrings and shoes. The designers had to use stepladders to get their models dressed, but the elephants were very well behaved. When all was ready, a photographer took pictures for a fashion magazine. The money the elephants made from their modeling was donated to some elephant causes.

1. From this paragraph, you can conclude that
- ○ A. elephants enjoy reading fashion magazines.
- ○ B. the clothing designers wanted to get attention.
- ○ C. many people bought the elephant clothes.
- ○ D. the elephants often work as fashion models.

2. Which sentence is most likely *not* true?
- ○ A. The elephants needed two pairs of shoes each.
- ○ B. The elephants chose the outfits they wore.
- ○ C. The designers used large amounts of fabric.
- ○ D. The elephants stood still while being dressed.

3. The title that best summarizes this paragraph is
- ○ A. Outsized Outfits.
- ○ B. Fashion Fun.
- ○ C. Elephant Causes.
- ○ D. Elephants as Models.

4. Reread the paragraph. Write a definition of the word **gigantic**.

_____

_____

Name _____ Date _____

Read the paragraph. Then answer the questions.

Matzeliger's Machine

Once, shoes were made entirely by hand. The hardest step
was connecting the upper part of a shoe to the innersole.
A worker had to stretch the leather over a wooden form called
a *last*. Jan Matzeliger changed all that in the 1880s.
He invented a lasting machine to do this difficult work.
<u>After that, shoes took a big step forward</u>! Matzeliger's
machine meant that many more shoes could be made in a day
than before and for less money. The price of shoes came down,
and more people could afford them.

1. The main idea of this paragraph is
- ○ A. once shoes were made by hand.
- ○ B. Matzeliger changed how shoes are made.
- ○ C. Jan Matzeliger was an inventor.
- ○ D. more people could now afford shoes.

2. Reread the paragraph. Write a detail that supports the main idea.

_____

_____

3. Which sentence is most likely *not* true?
- ○ A. More people bought new shoes.
- ○ B. People bought more shoes.
- ○ C. Matzeliger made money from his machine.
- ○ D. Shoemakers spent more time at work.

4. The underlined words in this paragraph are an example of figurative language called
- ○ A. metaphor.
- ○ B. personification.
- ○ C. simile.
- ○ D. hyperbole.

Name _____ Date _____

Read the paragraph. Then answer the questions.

Fort Christina

In 1638, a Swedish ship arrived in America. The immigrants aboard founded a community called Fort Christina. The Dutch soon took over this settlement, but not before the Swedes had built **snug** log cabins like those in their homeland. The cabins were made of notched logs carefully fitted together without nails. The walls were chinked with moss or clay, and the roofs were made of hardwood. Plentiful lumber made these easy-to-build cabins ideal for settlers. Log cabins became a symbol of the pioneer spirit.

1. The title that best summarizes this paragraph is
   ○ A. A Building Boom in 1638.
   ○ B. Contribution From the Dutch.
   ○ C. Building the Pioneer Spirit.
   ○ D. Log Cabins From the Swedish.

2. In this paragraph, the word **snug** means
   ○ A. small.   ○ B. cozy.
   ○ C. special.   ○ D. drafty.

3. From this paragraph, you can conclude that the Swedes
   ○ A. were good builders.
   ○ B. brought their own wood.
   ○ C. didn't like nails.
   ○ D. welcomed the Dutch.

4. Reread the paragraph. Write the main idea.

_____

_____

Name _____ **Date**_____

Read the paragraph. Then answer the questions.

Bridge Signs

Almost all bridges have them. I'm speaking of signs that say "Caution: Bridge Freezes Before Road." Many people wonder why it is that bridges freeze first. The answer is simple. A bridge is exposed to air both from above and below. When the temperature drops, heat accumulated in the bridge is released. A road, on the other hand, is only exposed to the environment from above. Heat **retained** in the ground actually provides insulation for roads so they take longer to freeze. So the important bridge signs help keep drivers safe.

1. Which phrase best reflects the writer's point of view?
   - ○ A. appreciative of the signs
   - ○ B. mystified by the signs
   - ○ C. leery of the signs

2. In this paragraph, the word **retained** means
   - ○ A. generated.
   - ○ B. given off.
   - ○ C. kept.
   - ○ D. blended.

3. The title that best summarizes this paragraph is
   - ○ A. Understanding Bridge Signs About Freezing.
   - ○ B. What Happens to Heat on Bridges.
   - ○ C. How Signs Keep Drivers Safe.
   - ○ D. Why Roads Keep Heat Longer.

4. From this paragraph, you can conclude that
   - ○ A. drivers usually speed up at bridges.
   - ○ B. road signs are easier to read than bridge signs.
   - ○ C. cars have more accidents on frozen bridges.
   - ○ D. passengers get cold driving over bridges.

Name _____ Date _____

Read the paragraph. Then answer the questions.

A President Preserves

President Franklin D. Roosevelt (1883–1945) loved trees. As a boy, he took great interest in his family's land in Hyde Park, New York. He learned the importance of preserving the land. Later, as president, he created job programs for unemployed people in the field of conservation. During the early 1930s, **catastrophic** dust storms had stripped away valuable soil in the Great Plains. Roosevelt's programs taught farmers how to protect the soil and how to plant trees as windbreaks to keep the soil from blowing away.

1. In this paragraph, the word **catastrophic** must mean
   - ○ A. drought-resistant.
   - ○ B. rather mild.
   - ○ C. really disastrous.
   - ○ D. greatly welcomed.

2. Which sentence is most likely *not* true?
   - ○ A. Roosevelt's programs helped farmers.
   - ○ B. Roosevelt's programs helped the soil.
   - ○ C. Roosevelt's programs helped stop dust storms.
   - ○ D. Roosevelt's programs helped unemployed people.

3. From this paragraph, you can conclude that
   - ○ A. Roosevelt was unemployed.
   - ○ B. the dust storms affected food production.
   - ○ C. the 1930s were a time of prosperity.
   - ○ D. farmers welcomed the dust storms.

4. Reread the paragraph. Write the main idea.

   _____

   _____

Name _____ **Date**_____

Read the paragraph. Then answer the questions.

Snowy Ride

<u>You don't know winter if you haven't tried snowboarding</u>. This winter sport began about 50 years ago in Vermont. To many fans, snowboarding is a ride on a frozen wave. It is a combination of surfing and skiing that takes thrill seekers down snow-covered mountains. Many boarders also perform stunts such as soaring into the air in a maneuver called a half-pipe. Snowboarding became an Olympic sport in the 1998 Winter Games in Nagano, Japan.

1. The underlined words in this paragraph are an example of figurative language called
   - ○ A. metaphor.
   - ○ B. personification.
   - ○ C. simile.
   - ○ D. hyperbole.

2. The title that best summarizes this paragraph is
   - ○ A. Doing the Half-Pipe.
   - ○ B. The Thrill of Snowboarding.
   - ○ C. A Vermont Sport.
   - ○ D. At the Winter Olympics.

3. The word that best reflects the writer's point of view is
   - ○ A. startled.
   - ○ B. convinced.
   - ○ C. disenchanted.

4. Reread the paragraph. Find and write an example of a metaphor.

_____

_____

Name _____ Date_____

Read the paragraph. Then answer the questions.

Pets for People

People have been living with **domesticated** animals for thousands of years. For example, dogs and people go back about 14,000 years. Believe me, dogs are "man's best friend." Cats have been around for a long time, too. The ancient Egyptians thought of cats as gods. People should remember that, because most cats today think of themselves as gods! Both children and adults should have pets. Birds, rabbits, and some types of fish are popular pets. I don't think they're as satisfying as dogs and cats, though.

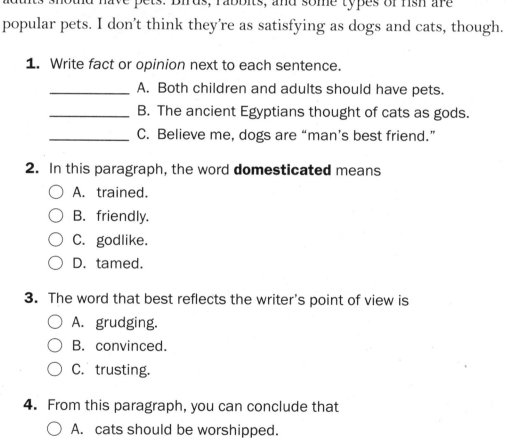

1. Write *fact* or *opinion* next to each sentence.
    _____ A. Both children and adults should have pets.
    _____ B. The ancient Egyptians thought of cats as gods.
    _____ C. Believe me, dogs are "man's best friend."

2. In this paragraph, the word **domesticated** means
    ○ A. trained.
    ○ B. friendly.
    ○ C. godlike.
    ○ D. tamed.

3. The word that best reflects the writer's point of view is
    ○ A. grudging.
    ○ B. convinced.
    ○ C. trusting.

4. From this paragraph, you can conclude that
    ○ A. cats should be worshipped.
    ○ B. rabbits have been pets for thousands of years.
    ○ C. pets have worked well for people.
    ○ D. fish are more popular pets than birds.

Name _____ Date_____

Read the paragraph. Then answer the questions.

Ikebana

Many people put flowers in a vase, but in Japan arranging flowers is **deemed** an art. It is called *ikebana* and has been practiced for about 500 years. Japanese teens often study flower arranging in school, and professional arrangers spend years mastering the art. Only a few flowers are used in an arrangement. These are carefully chosen to make a graceful composition. The tallest flower represents heaven, the shortest flower is for earth, and the one in the middle stands for humans. Most homes in Japan have a special place where flower arrangements are displayed.

1. Fill in the correct circle to show whether each statement is a fact or an inference.

   Fact   Inference
   ○   ○   A. *Ikebana* reflects an appreciation of beauty.
   ○   ○   B. The Japanese have practiced *ikebana* for 500 years.
   ○   ○   C. Much thought goes into a Japanese arrangement.
   ○   ○   D. Students learn about *ikebana* in school.

2. The title that best summarizes this paragraph is
   ○ A. Meanings of Flowers.   ○ B. Japanese Flower Arranging.
   ○ C. The Art of Flowers.   ○ D. A Graceful Composition.

3. From this paragraph, you can conclude that
   ○ A. flower arrangements are part of Japanese life.
   ○ B. the Japanese try to save on the use of flowers.
   ○ C. everyone in Japan has a garden.
   ○ D. flowers are chosen for their similar size.

4. In this paragraph, the word **deemed** means
   ○ A. donated.   ○ B. designed.
   ○ C. organized.   ○ D. considered.

Name _____ **Date**_____

Read the paragraph. Then answer the questions.

Ears at Work

Scientists have been learning more about ears. Until recently, most people thought both ears did the same work. However, studies have now shown that the right and left ear **process** sound differently. That's important research. If you are listening to someone speaking, your right ear is responding. If you are listening to music, your left ear is more attuned. Researchers think this new information is important in helping people with hearing loss. For example, a student with hearing loss in the right ear might need more help in school because the right ear is critical to learning situations.

1. From this paragraph, you can conclude that
   - ○ A. people really don't need two ears.
   - ○ B. the left ear is important to musicians.
   - ○ C. the right ear is larger than the left ear.
   - ○ D. the left and right ear are interchangeable.

2. The main idea of this paragraph is
   - ○ A. the left ear and the right ear.
   - ○ B. using the right ear for learning.
   - ○ C. how the left ear responds.
   - ○ D. what studies show about ears.

3. In this paragraph, the word **process** means
   - ○ A. continue. ○ B. treat.
   - ○ C. proceed. ○ D. erase.

4. Write *fact* or *opinion* next to each sentence.
   - _____ A. If you are listening to music, your left ear is more attuned.
   - _____ B. Until recently, most people thought both ears did the same work.
   - _____ C. That's important research.

Name _____ **Date** _____

Read the paragraph. Then answer the questions.

Over They Go

Niagara Falls is known for people who like to, well, go over the edge. The first mindless daredevil was Annie Edson Taylor in 1901. Bobby Leach went over in 1911, breaking not only his jaw but both kneecaps as well. Some of the next attempts didn't fare well at all. While Roger Woodward survived his trip over the falls in 1960, he never meant to go in the first place. He had a boating accident. Two people in one barrel made it over safely in 1989. Two more in a plastic capsule succeeded in 1995. So, who's next?

1. Which phrase best reflects the writer's point of view?
   - ○ A. disapproving of these actions
   - ○ B. sorry about these actions
   - ○ C. startled by these actions

2. The title that best summarizes this paragraph is
   - ○ A. Bobby Leach Breaks Jaw and Kneecaps.
   - ○ B. Going Over Niagara Falls.
   - ○ C. Plastic Capsule Rides Successfully.
   - ○ D. First Over Was Annie Edson Taylor.

3. Which of these sentences is most likely *not* true?
   - ○ A. Going over Niagara Falls is dangerous.
   - ○ B. Going over the falls is difficult.
   - ○ C. Many people have been injured going over the falls.
   - ○ D. Boats are the best way to go over the falls.

4. Reread the paragraph. Write the writer's opinion about going over Niagara Falls. Then write a fact that the writer gives.

_____

_____

Name _____ Date _____

Read the paragraph. Then answer the questions.

Oil History

People have used oil since early times. Ancient cultures learned that oil was sticky and useful for binding things together. They also noted that oil kept water out. For example, the Sumerians used the oil in asphalt to keep mosaics on walls and in floors. The people of Mesopotamia used the oil in bitumen to seal the joints in wooden boats. Other groups found that oil burned well to create light. Throughout the ages, hundreds of other uses for oil were discovered.

1. The main idea of this paragraph is
   ○ A. the Sumerians used oil as glue.
   ○ B. oil has sticky qualities.
   ○ C. when burned, oil creates light.
   ○ D. people have used oil through the ages.

2. Find and write a detail that supports the main idea.

   _____

   _____

3. From this paragraph, you can conclude that
   ○ A. oil is a recent discovery.
   ○ B. oil has limited uses for civilizations.
   ○ C. oil has long been valuable to people.
   ○ D. oil is mostly found in asphalt.

4. Which sentence is most likely *not* true?
   ○ A. The Mesopotamians were sailors.
   ○ B. People were always looking for new uses of oil.
   ○ C. The Sumerians decorated their buildings.
   ○ D. Ancient cultures had big oil refineries.

1. Main Idea   2. Details   3. Draw Conclusions   4. Inference

Name _____   **Date**_____

Read the paragraph. Then answer the questions.

Home Styles

No doubt you have read about exciting new buildings designed by famous architects. Some of these are spectacular. However, many homes are built in a **vernacular** style. This means their design is traditional to the group that builds them. For example, the Pueblo in the Southwest used adobe homes to shield people from the sun. Many pioneers cut the prairie soil into blocks to build sod houses on the treeless plains. In wooded areas, settlers put up log houses similar to those they had used back in Europe.

1. In this paragraph, the word **vernacular** must mean
   - ○ A. particular design.
   - ○ B. contemporary model.
   - ○ C. spectacular plan.
   - ○ D. native to a culture.

2. Write *fact* or *opinion* next to each sentence.
   - _____ A. However, many homes are built in a vernacular style.
   - _____ B. Some of them are spectacular.
   - _____ C. This means their design is traditional to the group that builds them.

3. The main idea of this paragraph is
   - ○ A. sod houses on the treeless prairie.
   - ○ B. adobe homes in the Southwest.
   - ○ C. homes that reflect native traditions.
   - ○ D. exciting new designs for buildings.

4. Which sentence is most likely *not* true?
   - ○ A. The environment affects how people build homes.
   - ○ B. Immigrants built homes in familiar styles.
   - ○ C. Only architects like exciting new buildings.
   - ○ D. Sod houses were not necessary in wooded areas.

1. Context Clues   2. Fact & Opinion   3. Main Idea   4. Inference

Comprehension Skills: 40 Short Passages for Close Reading, Grade 6 © 2012 by Linda Ward Beech,

Name _____ Date _____

Read the paragraph. Then answer the questions.

It's the Law

<u>Sometimes laws can seem as silly as a clown's clothes</u>. Usually, these are laws that were once made for a reason but are no longer needed. Here are some **absurd** laws from Canada. In Saskatoon, you cannot catch fish with your hands. In Calgary, it's against the law to toss snowballs without the mayor's permission. Children can't eat ice cream cones on the streets of Ottawa on Sundays. Places in the U.S. have strange laws, too. Some make as much sense as a talking turtle.

1. The underlined words in this paragraph are an example of figurative language called
   - ○ A. metaphor.
   - ○ B. personification.
   - ○ C. simile.
   - ○ D. hyperbole.

2. The title that best summarizes this paragraph is
   - ○ A. Silly Laws From Canada.
   - ○ B. Ask the Mayor for Permission.
   - ○ C. Clownish Laws.
   - ○ D. Strange Laws in the U.S.

3. The word that best reflects the writer's point of view is
   - ○ A. thrilled.
   - ○ B. unamused.
   - ○ C. sympathetic.

4. In this paragraph, the word **absurd** means
   - ○ A. abused.
   - ○ B. ridiculous.
   - ○ C. random.
   - ○ D. outdated.

Name _____ Date _____

Read the paragraph. Then answer the questions.

Patterns in Nature

Many living things have internal clocks. These are daily patterns known as circadian rhythms. One of the most common is the pattern of sleep that humans follow. Certain flowers patterns, too. These flowers open and close their petals on specific schedules. For example, dandelions open at nine in the morning. People should get rid of dandelions because they're weeds. A morning glory opens at 10 A.M., and a water lily at 11. My favorite flower is the California poppy. Its petals open at 1 P.M.

1. Write *fact* or *opinion* next to each sentence.

    _____ A. Many living things have internal clocks.

    _____ B. My favorite flower is the California poppy.

    _____ C. People should get rid of dandelions because they're weeds.

2. From this paragraph, you can conclude that circadian rhythms
    - ○ A. all have to do with sleep.
    - ○ B. are the same in all living things.
    - ○ C. are all about when flowers open.
    - ○ D. affect how living things act.

3. Which sentence is most likely *not* true?
    - ○ A. Poppies open early in the afternoon.
    - ○ B. Many flowers close their petals at night.
    - ○ C. Circadian rhythms affect when people sleep.
    - ○ D. All flowers open their petals on a schedule.

4. Reread the paragraph. Write the main idea.

    _____

    _____

Comprehension Skills: 40 Short Passages for Close Reading, Grade 6 © 2012 by Linda Ward Beech, Scholastic Teaching Resources

Name _____ Date _____

Read the paragraph. Then answer the questions.

A Hot Topic

You're probably aware of extreme sports such as
dangling from bungee cords over cliffs. But have
you heard about extreme ironing? The first Extreme
Ironing World Championships took place in Germany
in 2002. Top contestants included ironists with names
such as Starch and Steam. They pressed clothes while
scaling a wall, hanging from tree branches, and balancing
on ironing boards. No kidding! Since then, ironists have attacked
wrinkled clothing all over the world. They've ironed while
riding bicycles, scuba diving, and even climbing Mount Everest.
Wow! Starch manufacturers must be thrilled. <u>Ironing is the most
versatile sport of all!</u>

1. Which word best reflects the writer's point of view about extreme ironing?
- ○ A. bored
- ○ B. offended
- ○ C. amused

2. A title that best summarizes this paragraph is
- ○ A. Extreme Ironing Antics.
- ○ B. Pressing Clothes.
- ○ C. Starch and Steam.
- ○ D. Champions at Work.

3. The underlined words in this paragraph are an example of
- ○ A. metaphor.   ○ B. personification.
- ○ C. simile.   ○ D. hyperbole.

4. Reread the paragraph. Write a conclusion you can make about extreme ironing.

_____

_____

Name _____ **Date** _____

Read the paragraph. Then answer the questions.

Check the Calendar

When the calendar says April 1, you should be careful.
Someone may play a silly joke on you because it is April Fool's
Day. This day is celebrated in the United States, France,
England, and Scotland. Putting salt in the sugar bowl is a
popular trick in the U.S. A **prank** people use in France is to pin
a paper fish on someone else's back without getting caught.
The person wearing the fish is called a *poisson d'avril*, or April
fish. In England, a person who is tricked is called a *noddie* or a
gawby. An April fool in Scotland is a *cuckoo* or a *gowk*.

1. Fill in the correct circle to show whether each statement is a fact or an inference.

Fact **Inference**

◯ ◯ A. April Fool's is on the first day of April.

◯ ◯ B. A paper fish prank is popular in France.

◯ ◯ C. A *noddie* or a *gawby* is an English April fool.

◯ ◯ D. People enjoy playing silly tricks on others.

2. The title that best summarizes this paragraph is

◯ A. Paper Fish in France. ◯ B. Don't Be a Noddie.

◯ C. April Fool's Day Jokes. ◯ D. Salt in the Sugar Bowl.

3. Write *fact* or *opinion* next to each sentence.

_____ A. An April fool in Scotland is a *cuckoo* or *gowk*.

_____ B. Putting salt in the sugar bowl is a popular trick in the U.S.

_____ C. When the calendar says April 1, you should be careful.

4. Reread the paragraph. Write the meaning of the word **prank**.

_____

_____

Comprehension Skills: 40 Short Passages for Close Reading: Grade 6 © 2012 by Linda Ward Beech, Scholastic Teaching Resources

Name _____ **Date** _____

Read the paragraph. Then answer the questions.

Pay Attention to Prices

The price for an ice cream cone is posted in a shop window. You decide to buy one. "Would you like a topping?" asks the clerk. You decide to have one. The price of your cone has just gone up. A new word for this practice is *shrouding*. Economists think that shrouding affects much of what people buy today. It's sneaky. In a restaurant people pay extra for bottled rather than tap water. A new car has many features that add to its cost. If you buy tickets for an event over the phone, there is an additional charge. How can a consumer avoid shrouding? One answer is to think carefully about the value of things before buying.

> ## Ice Cream Cones
> $1.50 – Maybe

1. From this paragraph, you can conclude that
   - ○ A. all ice cream cones are the same price.
   - ○ B. prices of things are higher than many people realize.
   - ○ C. it's better to drink bottled water than tap water.
   - ○ D. it's worthwhile to order tickets over the phone.

2. The word that best reflects the writer's point of view is
   - ○ A. enthralled.
   - ○ B. instructive.
   - ○ C. saddened.

3. The main idea of this paragraph is
   - ○ A. why ice cream cones cost more.
   - ○ B. when bottled water adds to prices.
   - ○ C. how shrouding affects prices.
   - ○ D. costs for ordering over the phone.

4. Reread the paragraph. Find and write an opinion.

   _____

   _____

1. Draw Conclusions 2. Point of View 3. Main Idea 4. Fact & Opinion

Name _____ Date _____

Read the paragraph. Then answer the questions.

Funny Phrase

The words *flotsam and jetsam* are often used to refer to the unfortunate in society. However, these words once referred to **cargo** found floating in water. Flotsam was cargo from a wrecked ship. Jetsam was cargo that was purposely thrown overboard either to lighten the ship's load or to keep the goods from going down with the ship. Jetsam belonged to the ship's owner. Anything that was flotsam belonged to the government.

1. The title that best summarizes this paragraph is
   - ○ A. Society's Less Fortunate.
   - ○ B. Learning About Flotsam.
   - ○ C. Story of Flotsam and Jetsam.
   - ○ D. Cargo From Shipwrecks.

2. In this paragraph, the word **cargo** means
   - ○ A. cars on a boat.
   - ○ B. a ship's freight.
   - ○ C. equipment from a ship.
   - ○ D. oil leaked from a ship.

3. Which of these sentences is most likely *not* true?
   - ○ A. Cargo became flotsam by accident.
   - ○ B. Society's unfortunate were tossed in the sea.
   - ○ C. Cargo became jetsam to help a ship go faster.
   - ○ D. Cargo became jetsam in shallow water.

4. Reread the paragraph. Write the main idea.

   _____

   _____

Comprehension Skills: 40 Short Passages for Close Reading, Grade 6 © 2012 by Linda Ward Beech, Scholastic Teaching Resources

1. Summarize   2. Context Clues   3. Inference   4. Main Idea

Answers

page 7:
1. D
2. Answers will vary.
3. C
4. C

page 8:
1. A
2. C
3. B
4. C

page 9:
1. B
2. D
3. A
4. Answers will vary.

page 10:
1. D
2. C
3. A
4. Answers will vary but should reflect the text.

page 11:
1. C
2. C
3. C
4. A

page 12:
1. A. Fact
   B. Opinion
   C. Fact
2. That was an excellent time for talented people.
3. B
4. D

page 13:
1. A. Fact
   B. Inference
   C. Fact
   D. Inference
2. C
3. B
4. B

page 14:
1. D
2. C
3. D
4. The writer thinks letterboxing is very cool. Most letterbox fans carry their own stamps.

page 15:
1. C
2. Answers will vary.
3. B
4. D

page 16:
1. C
2. C
3. D
4. The tower, called Pharos, was a mighty giant.

page 17:
1. C
2. B
3. A
4. A. Fact
   B. Opinion
   C. Fact

page 18:
1. B
2. C
3. C
4. C

page 19:
1. A
2. C
3. A
4. A

page 20:
1. A. Fact
   B. Opinion
   C. Opinion
2. A
3. C
4. B

page 21:
1. B
2. B
3. A. Fact
   B. Opinion
   C. Fact
4. B

page 22:
1. B
2. Answers will vary.
3. C
4. A

page 23:
1. D
2. B
3. D
4. Possible: skeptical

page 24:
1. B
2. A. Opinion
   B. Fact
   C. Opinion
3. B
4. B

page 25:
1. A
2. C
3. C
4. Answers will vary but should reflect the text.

page 26:
1. B
2. C
3. A. Fact
   B. Opinion
   C. Fact
4. A

page 27:
1. A. Fact
   B. Fact
   C. Opinion
2. A
3. C
4. A large granite head looks out of Thunderhead Mountain in South Dakota.

page 28:
1. A. Fact
   B. Inference
   C. Inference
   D. Fact
2. B
3. C
4. That's a remarkable achievement!

page 29:
1. B
2. B
3. D
4. Possible: very large; enormous

page 30:
1. B
2. Answers will vary.
3. D
4. B

page 31:
1. D
2. B
3. A
4. Answers will vary but should reflect the text.

page 32:
1. A
2. C
3. A
4. C

page 33:
1. C
2. C
3. B
4. Answers will very but should reflect the text.

page 34:
1. D
2. B
3. B
4. snowboarding is a ride on a frozen wave

Answers

page 35:
1. A. Opinion
   B. Fact
   C. Opinion
2. D
3. B
4. C

page 36:
1. A. Inference
   B. Fact
   C. Inference
   D. Fact
2. B
3. A
4. D

page 37:
1. B
2. D
3. B
4. A. Fact
   B. Fact
   C. Opinion

page 38:
1. A
2. B
3. D
4. Possible: The writer thinks going over the falls is for mindless daredevils. Fact: Two people in one barrel made it over safely in 1989.

page 39:
1. D
2. Answers will vary.
3. C
4. D

page 40:
1. D
2. A. Fact
   B. Opinion
   C. Fact
3. C
4. C

page 41:
1. C
2. A
3. B
4. B

page 42:
1. A. Fact
   B. Opinion
   C. Opinion
2. D
3. D
4. Answers will vary but should reflect the text.

page 43:
1. C
2. A
3. D
4. Answers will vary but should reflect the text.

page 44:
1. A. Fact
   B. Fact
   C. Fact
   D. Inference
2. C
3. A. Fact
   B. Fact
   C. Opinion
4. Possible: trick

page 45:
1. B
2. B
3. C
4. It's sneaky.

page 46:
1. C
2. B
3. B
4. Answers will vary but should reflect the text.

Comprehension Skills: 40 Short Passages for Close Reading, Grade 6 © 2012 by Linda Ward Beech, Scholastic Teaching Resources